Be Wild

Amazing Animal Behaviors to Inspire Growing Humans

Leigh Crandall

illustrated by
Angela Edmonds

Albert Whitman & Company
Chicago, Illinois

For Marcelo—LC

A special thanks to the menagerie of animals
I have had in my life—AE

Library of Congress Cataloging-in-Publication data
is on file with the publisher.
Text copyright © 2023 by Leigh Crandall
Illustrations copyright © 2023 by Albert Whitman & Company
Illustrations by Angela Edmonds
First published in the United States of America in 2023
by Albert Whitman & Company
ISBN 978-0-8075-0628-8 (hardcover)
ISBN 978-0-8075-0629-5 (ebook)
Printed in China
10 9 8 7 6 5 4 3 2 1 CJ 28 27 26 25 24 23

Design by Rick DeMonico

For more information about Albert Whitman & Company,
visit our website at www.albertwhitman.com.

Some adults tell you not to behave like an animal.

But why not? Elephants and dolphins are great at greetings. Barn owls are good listeners, and warthogs and octopuses have eating habits we could all use.

Animals communicate with each other, work together, and have some healthy habits. There is a lot we can learn from them.

So, go ahead.

Be wild!

Be wild like a dolphin—introduce yourself!

Bottlenose dolphins have special melodies called signature whistles. They use these whistles to introduce themselves when they meet new dolphins. Each whistle is unique and helps dolphins recognize others. Dolphins can remember each other for more than twenty years.

A friendly introduction makes a big impression.

Be wild like an elephant— say hello!

When African elephants see other members of their herd, they make rumbling noises that mean "Hi there! Good to see you!" Elephants also greet friends and family by touching and sniffing each other with their trunks. Sometimes they even wrap their trunks together, the elephant version of a handshake.

Be wild like an orangutan— make your bed!

If you think making your bed is a lot of work, imagine being an orangutan. Orangutans build new beds in the treetops every day.

First, an orangutan finds a sturdy spot high up in a tree's boughs. It weaves a base for its nest from large branches, then adds smaller branches to make a kind of mattress. An orangutan may also gather leafy limbs together to make a pillow or a blanket.

Sleeping in trees helps keep orangutans safe from predators, though scientists think the main reason orangutans make beds is simply to have comfy places to sleep—just like you.

Be wild like a polar bear— ask nicely!

When a polar bear wants to share another bear's meal, it asks calmly and respectfully. The hungry bear slowly approaches, walks in a circle around the food, then touches the other bear's nose with its own. This works almost every time, just like saying please.

Be wild like a honeybee— use teamwork!

Tens of thousands of bees live together in a hive, and each one pitches in to look for food, make honey, and support the queen bee, who is busy laying eggs.

Bees even help each other find the best flowers for gathering nectar and pollen. When one bee discovers the perfect flower, it does a "waggle dance," a little jig that tells other bees where it is.

Be wild like a beaver—wipe your feet!

After a busy day of dam-building in rivers and ponds, beavers go home to lodges they build from sticks and mud.

A lodge has an area just past the entrance for drying off and cleaning wet paws. This helps the grass and leaves in beaver bedrooms stay dry and cozy.

Be wild like a barn owl— be a good listener!

Can you hear a whisper from across a room? You could if you were a barn owl.

An owl's hearing can be ten times more sensitive than a human's because of its special ears, located at different heights on either side of the owl's head.

This helps the owl figure out exactly where sounds are coming from, which is important for hunting. Owls can pinpoint even the tiniest scuffle of a mouse beneath the snow.

Be wild like a hippo—
wear sunscreen!

Sun protection is important, even for tough-skinned hippopotamuses. Luckily, hippo sweat works just like sunscreen to keep these animals from getting a sunburn. It also acts as medicine to help stop infections and as a bug repellent to keep mosquitoes and flies away.

Be wild like an octopus— try new foods!

Each of an octopus's eight arms is lined with suckers that not only stick to things, but also taste them. When an octopus is curious about what a new food might be like, it touches it with its arms to try the flavor before eating it.

Be wild like a warthog— sit down to eat !

Warthogs graze on grass and plants, using their snouts and sharp tusks to dig for roots. When they are ready to eat, warthogs fold their front legs and kneel while they enjoy their meals.

Be wild like a sloth—eat slowly!

A sloth never rushes. Three-toed sloths are the slowest animals on the planet. They crawl slowly, blink slowly, and even eat slowly.

It can take a sloth a whole month to digest one meal of leaves.

Be wild like a humpback whale— pass the food!

Humpback whales work together at mealtime by bubble-net feeding, a way to share food. Several whales swim in spirals beneath a school of fish and release air bubbles. The ring of bubbles traps the fish inside like a net, then the whales swim through, gulping down fish as they go.

Be wild like a bird— take a bath!

All birds take baths, but not every bird bathes the same way.
Bluebirds go for a dip in shallow water, like a backyard birdbath. They sit with their bellies in the water then flick their wings and roll from side to side to get wet. When bluebirds are done with their baths, they shake the extra water off their feathers and fly away.

Wild turkeys take dust baths to keep their feathers smooth and shiny. They rub their bodies against the ground until they are covered with powdery dirt, which keeps the feathers from getting too greasy or matted. When turkeys shake off the dust, pesky parasites and dry skin fall off too.

Be wild like a jackrabbit—wash your ears and feet!

Black-tailed jackrabbits' ears can be as long as six inches, more than double the size of adult human ears. They use their large feet to push those big ears forward to lick them clean with their tongues. Then, jackrabbits lick their feet clean, too.

Be wild like a chimpanzee—
brush your hair and clean your teeth!

Chimpanzees keep their hair free of knots, dirt, and bugs by letting other chimps groom them with their fingers and mouths. Chimpanzees can spend several hours a day grooming each other and have even been known to use twigs like toothpicks to clean each other's teeth.

Be wild like a sea otter— get ready for bed!

Sea otters love water so much they even sleep there.

But first, they do a sort of bedtime routine, lying on their backs and snuggling up in groups called rafts. They wrap themselves in kelp, a kind of giant seaweed, to keep from floating away. Sometimes otters even hold each other's paws to make sure no one gets lost while they are sleeping.

Be wild like a koala— get a good night's sleep!

Koalas get a good day's sleep, too, snoozing up to twenty-two hours every day. Resting for so long helps koalas conserve energy and digest the pound of eucalyptus leaves they eat each day.

When they are ready for bed, koalas tuck themselves into comfy forks in the tree branches high above the forest floor, close their eyes, and fade off to sleep.

Author's Note

Animals are not so different from you and me. One of the best ways to make sure they continue to be wild is to learn how to protect them and their habitats.

Children's Reference Books:

Judge, Lita. *Play in the Wild: How Baby Animals Like to Have Fun*. New York: Roaring Brook Press, 2020.

Spelman, Lucy. *National Geographic Animal Encyclopedia 2nd Edition*. Washington, D.C.: National Geographic, 2021.

Zommer, Yuval. *The Big Book of Beasts*. New York: Thames and Hudson, 2017.